EAST SIDE SOLITUDE

poems, prose, and illustrations by

Asyia Gover

Finishing Line Press
Georgetown, Kentucky

EAST SIDE SOLITUDE

Publisher: Leah Huete de Maines
Editor: Christen Kincaid
Cover Art: Cheyenne Phoenix Wing-Lawrence
Author Photo: Asyia Gover
Cover Design: Elizabeth Maines McCleavy

Order online: www.finishinglinepress.com
            also available on amazon.com

Author inquiries and mail orders:
Finishing Line Press
PO Box 1626
Georgetown, Kentucky 40324
USA

Contents

東側 (higashigawa)

Seeds of the ancestors' anger were raised
by the scorching sun each day, baking the earthen buildings
once more, the crusty, dry nostrils therein.
"Stop!!"—a scorpion at less than arm's length
poised to strike; the last time a stranger watched his back.
By night, the oracle alone with the ghosts in the attic.
By morning, the voices drifted up again:
curse words exchanged with the rooster on the roof.
Cloves, anise and bay leaf riding the steam from rice,
simmering curry, flame-licked beef,
small teeth sank into hot shawarma—
cool turquoise water and the flash of the blade,
day trips to Abu Dhabi with the trust fund children
and their faithful entourage, and the salt of sweat,
and the luster of honey. The sharpness of sandalwood
and frankincense in the land of the two holy mosques,
the men of the house passing hashish around adult conversations.
The boy with the soccer field in his back yard,
how the tender seed brought the ever-blossom
of friendship, long after their last game.

The sour steam from warm soymilk,
thin skin stretched across the bowl.
Watching my face intently, my relatives
had finished eating long ago, a reminder
not to look at myself through irrelevant eyes.
Stiff left hand fingers fumbled the chopsticks.
The twin towers alight on TV; the adults &
their discourse in a language I don't speak.
Alone & scowling in an overexposed photo
atop the Great Wall, the stubborn trees growing sideways
on steep, rocky slopes; the quantum entanglement
of ancient bones. 15 years later, my brother
and I, back to back at the same scene.
I am sick in the back of a taxi
leaving the floating restaurant in Shanghai.

This hunger can only be sated in secret.
Fire claws through my core and I am face up;
my gaze follows jagged peaks crowned
with sacred stones; neck nearly snaps
at the summit. Over a long & dark night we pass
through the ship locks of the Three Gorges Dam.
Jungle of concrete & rooftop trees in the south,
dense smog like skin on sky in the north,
thick space, the scissors confiscated at SeaTac
and the closing, again, of this gate.

Been a long time since the dim rooms,
tinny cheers, Ric Flair triumphant on TV.
Now no applause, no signs, just the colors of
sunrise on skin, and sap. Every flower has endured
the rain at times. How quickly the children
grew and turned their thorns on each other.
What choice but to harden the eyes?
Long gone are the days of laughter in the wind,
large and small hands together, he and his brother holding
the string, looking up. The space is getting thicker.
Gold leaves streaming from the trees,
a reminder that he will not grow roots here.
Lads with million-dollar names on horseback, meanwhile
sweat seeps into the collar under his blazer, the
stagnant air, his feet stiff after the 15th hour.
He's the man with the clipboard that everyone
has a question for, the second-most accomplished
man in New York this evening. Later
at night he is the man in a dirty overshirt,
utterly alone, who must sprint into a cruel destiny,
must use a power that no one has learned
to control yet. Memphis is sinking.
How quickly he hardened the eyes.

Sticky fingers pluck the ponderosa bark from the tree,
vanilla scent on my skin and released into air. Our
ancestors' anger grew up from the earth and became
these basalt columns peeking out from
under crumbling topsoil. I clamber from
jagged peak to peak as the spray pelts my face.
Elusive flow of inspiration, the river is swollen
with spring, the metallic grit washed down
from Silver Mountain, slag swirling below
Lake Coeur d'Alene, rapids turning just beneath
the Monroe Street Bridge. Each year we await
the first soul reported sacrificed to the cycle
of death and rebirth, the search and rescue team
downstream but coming up empty. The relentless current
of life surging through raw elements, Mother Nature
pregnant everywhere. When the water level lowers,
the season of mosquitos, and heat stroke. The eyes dry,
the lips pale, the back of the car where I am face up;
each morning I awake to the scent of sunny, dry
wood, and rust. The Children of the Sun
and their forgotten fishing camp at the shore
in Peaceful Valley; the shallow skinnydipping
spot, before houses went up on the north bank.
Only a few breaths before the season of
smoke; the Columbia Basin becomes a campfire
but wrong, apocalyptic, and I visit wistfully
the river, see how between three waters the traffic
of life keeps moving west. I must join the flow,
although I've come upstream before and will yet,
I pack up the Explorer and follow the sunset.

Blow by Blow

Late in the morning, the sun was there, somewhere, behind the bowl of mountains and clouds. The blackberry thicket surrounded us like a scratchy blanket. No one else could hear the laughs that burst unexpectedly, power from my solar plexus. Those joyful vibrations masked more subtle movements below us, the quantum entanglement of roots. I was surprised and a little scared by the warmth that bubbled up where our skins connected. Smoke drifted out of my sunroof. I kept my eyes on the joint, back and forth.

Beyond the haze, the pink and blue lights set a hallucinatory stage. I watched her, waist to shoulders, half a bottle of gin deep, sip her shitty well drink. Her breath shook harder than her hands, side to side. At the tables around us the scene repeated half a dozen times—two young women playing at sisterhood, passing awkward glances, holding on desperately to a thread of intimacy. A reminder that every date must come to an end. Everywhere the fog of intoxication hung thick. I was quite stoned and stayed silent, hardened the eyes. She was quite stoned and she couldn't shut up. I couldn't stop hearing her.

I imagine the surface of Lake Whatcom, perfectly still, slate tableau with my face reflected inside. What do you think happens to your shed skins once they sink through my sleek façade? You have me contained in your arms, but you're dreaming of whose embrace envelops whom, how I envelop you when I stretch out. Waves are set off and rebound endlessly against the inside of my shell, tides of life pulsing through raw elements. Three waters struggle to hold balance within me as you splash like a child. Throat still tightly closed, you'll never know how I make treasure out of torture, pleasure from your poison. I take in the nutrients and exhale.

It hurt, truly, to extinguish my own flame. I wonder, but I know, why I had not done it long before. The lingering scent of five spice, frankincense draws me into vivid reminiscence—I light joint after joint, but I cannot cover it up. I am tired of being put out halfway through, tired of clinging to the wick, tired of brushing off ashes, tired of falling casually from a slack hand. I must stop envisioning your face, eyes wide, drinking me in as I drink you. Cedarwood and sandalwood sparks turn to embers, and these watchful eyes must watch my own back. When I ignite this love in my mind, it burns at both ends.

I can't break the glass of illusion for you, and I found it funny that you'd accuse me of doing so. In those eternal moments, when my lips pressed into your chest, when our left hands connected, or when we linked our breaths, I was casting no spell. Think instead about the precious magic of being yourself, of leaving that half-vulnerability on the other side of the sunroof. The infinite and terrifying experience of surrendering to one's own wholeness. Hashish and adult conversations. This is what I wanted to share when I handed you the pipe.

alchemical hysterical

After Lilac City, I prefer
the thrill of drunk riding, the
game of hanging on with
slack hands like
flame clinging to the tip
of a candle on the move,
riding out the struggle—
no matter where the
road goes, no matter how
the vision blurs, how
the ears become hollow
on the ascent to fucked up.
Shortly now we round
a corner, a turn I didn't want
to take, crossfaded, someone
tailing us relentlessly
at the edge of the state,
the roads diverge again.

What burns at both ends like
a hunger that can only be
sated in secret? The drive
to consume sometimes
overpowers the anise, cloves,
sweat and regret—
what's really
on my palate.
Deeper and deeper, the
lips, the tongue, the teeth
sink into hot flesh, the
gnawing awareness that
sometimes what I crave
will kill me,
but that's a topic
to chew
and swallow.

Ford Explorer seat embrace
catch me as I clench,
shivers rip through my back,
fire clawing through my core,
clattering the teeth
like in those dreams—
your dim light, crystallized
flame without heat—
familiar fear of chaos
shows in repeated plunges
into the deep,
the shift and the shudder,
Explorer in gear,
the mud-splattered sides; I'd
never looked under the hood,
only heard the rumble roar.

———————————————

How many hours spent
beside the stage, or facing it
from a distance, swaying
amusedly side-to-side,
your smile a welcome
sight in the crowd, inviting
like a tall glass of ice water?
Is it true that
the lights and the stares,
salt of sweat isn't for you,
or are you waiting for that
elusive flow of inspiration?
Love, like water, seeks
the lowest places; again
and again your open palm
is met with a fist:
empty, tight,
dry.

Light passes through
the water—

mirror's surface
transverse, and
reflected upside-down
before it reaches your
eyes, sometimes skipping
realignment. The words
rebound endlessly, come
out upside-down, this
half-vulnerability
seems right to you—
hands reach out
upside-down, bringing
you so close,
having never been
so far away.

Slosh from side to side,
between three waters you
find your balance on the
tilted Explorer seat,
on the steep driveway
that would have you
cascading downhill, first
drop
on this emotional roller
coaster,
hear the last click;
exert your power to
externalize how sick
it feels right now,
to carry the tiniest vibrations,
shaking in place.

_____

Expertly arranged, the
shapes of his eyes,
blunt taper of his
fingertips evidence
exactly what was

meant for this creation.
The sculptor,
God,
speaks a whole
dialect with the twitch
of his tendons, clench in the
throat, invisible electricity
that he returns to the
earth with firm feet on
the ground, knees bent,
knuckles sharp, eyes wide
expressing exactly
the chaos &
the quiet façade.

Sighs of contempt
carve canyon walls,
pick scabs into channels
through which he labors to
circulate the energy—
breathe in,
breathe out—
before it reaches to
his fingertips, to his toes—
entangled into action,
faithful stone soldiers—
mouth will open but
often only
to spit back out
the poison trapped
in his lungs—
a string of lifestream
clinging to his lips.

Seated at the edge
of the bed, the
oracle begins to speak.
Born of jagged peaks and
bound with blood, his

mouth floods with
curses which wrack the
muscles with spasms
until the evil runs dry.
His voice has power
that no one has learned
to control yet.
Only the temple's sacred
stones know who
closes their ears in fear;
from the floor, palms up,
let me receive his plea.

———————————

Immobilized my own flame
although the warmth
radiates, how it aches, how
it claws through my core,
a reminder that light can
only flicker and dance so far
beyond these crystal walls—
of course you called first
when I'd finally let you go
like sparks into embers,
a sunburn's furious glow,
a streak of dazzling
light on the water.

The first
bubble bursts
your glassy guise
with a visible drawing up
from your waist to
shoulders, up
rising steam from the bottom
where our ancestors'
anger is planted and
grows, swirling circular mass
fogging the glass

emerging now, surfacing
scalding
throat still tightly closed.

Familiar screech,
tiny vibrations,
release when he plunges
headfirst in the cold,
dripping with steam,
lying back in the coals,
his spine becoming harder,
ugly metamorphosis,
jagged peaks in the sky—
no one would ask
what was there before
the shine and sharp edge
before the harvest blade,
he hardened the eyes,
the crushing stone.

Springtime on 546
5/12/20

I am so close to your hair that my lips, my fingertips tingle with magic—beeswax and coconut and shea. I savor every second in this hermetic basement suite, the nectar-scented morning light awaiting us outside. The silky warmth of skin on skin was so hard-won, the strands so meticulously wrapped up. I envelop you when I stretch out, my left palm holding your head. Breathe in the power from my solar plexus. I ask you what I smell like, and the response comes back muffled, low, rumbling through my breast, billowing in this dirty denim overshirt. I know exactly what you want when you press your face into my chest; I ask you again, and you lift your eyes from your reverie and speak up: salt, and honey.

5:30AM
We sip tea in the stillness and watch a palette's procession across my window: beryl, rose, gold, finally pewter and pearl. The looming Cascades to the east steal the first thirty minutes of each celestial show. Ten years ago it would have been the moonrise that I'd invite you to view over a well-worn background slope. I keep picking up and putting down the phone. We both struggle with faith in our own ways, like how nights promise to overtake days. I know you'll reach me through thickening space, because you're awake and thinking of me. Though neither the rainbows nor the lilacs in the back yard last, I am convinced that our flower does not become precious by wilting. Ten years from now, who knows against which gorges we'll see the moon?

SR 546
I wait for the pungence of dairy farms to pass on the way to paradise. The clouds are taunting me today with a coy blush on the cornflower blanket, bruises on thin soymilk skin. The best colors as usual peek out in the west; then a right turn I didn't want to take, and they are behind me. Driving into this bowl of mountains, I feel profoundly at home, although the jagged peaks punctuate the scene like a sickened dream. It's flirtatious, the essence of cedarwood and sandalwood, lilacs along the fence, flowers on mossy trees, a spring-green fringe. A reminder to hold on to the

precious magic of being myself, never mind how the other girls hated my denim and musk. I am radiating that which I wish to attract. Let all their faces be rubbed into it, they who dare taste the salt of my skin.

Count down

5/12
The space is getting thicker every second
from hills of fluffy comforter to wooden door
behind which, your deep tone echoes
& the last time I watched your back
two hours late to SeaTac
& now when I call your name: no response.

5/11
Paper bag packed, I write
with the juicy green chisel tip.
An adult conversation that I don't
know how to start. No
greeting card to say congratulations
& farewell at the same time.

5/10
I know you have your ways—
cloves & anise, cooking in honor
of the ancestors—five spice
& ginger. Impossible to know
whose embrace envelops whom—
steam & salt fill the room.

5/9
I will keep one underexposed photo
when the space becomes too thick
to cross—a reminder that these data
crystallize us, carefree without
the knowledge of which long look
at each other would be the last.

5/8
Crème brulée my shoulders—
I'm out at sea searching for
serenity, caught between three waters
I was praying for direction.

Nimble fingers clip lilacs
& dream of more strands to twist.

5/7
Hot leather pressing on the gathered
gold at my crown—the S40
sunroof a portal into which I twist
up the very last strands, entanglement—
braiding my hair
while we do ride or die shit.

5/6
One week since the last time
the world turned upside down
& a week before then, too.
Flame extinguished—
the relief hard-won,
this long & dark night.

5/5
I am radiating that
which I wish to attract.
I steep lilac brew with
my sorrow, assemble poetry
from our silence. I've grown
enough heart for us both.

5/4
Burlington streets mostly unchanged
since colonization, and here:
two lost souls with one bag
to burn & two cases to beat.
We're in deep, now—let me
be quick to flash the plastic.

5/3
Warning signs long gone, we
raced to a cruel destiny, burnt
at both ends, not the worst time

I'd faced an officer from the
passenger's seat, silent & furious,
my eyes always on your back.

5/2
Lilacs outside my window, &
my hands weaving arrangements
from the bounty of the earth. I left
flowers on your doorstep; heaven left
a rainbow at my back door, a
promise of quiet in chaos.

5/1
The sanctuary I wish I could share
with you: turquoise water, rooftop
gardens, silver & glass,
a black cat curled up in bed.
I'd take the fall if I could—
a welcome that never wears out.

4/30
Sleep & work come in
shifts, racing up & down I-5
now chasing my needs, now
chasing yours. One woman is
almost enough to deliver
you from cell to safety.

4/29
I see how sparks turn to
embers, how a room full of
gas ignites. Exchanging curse
words, cocksure, burnt
at both ends when the red &
blue body snatchers arrive.

4/28
I must take the plunge to find
out exactly what the fuck kind

of game we're playing. Been long
enough since I hardened the eyes,
my left hand met with a fist,
the last roller coaster click.

4/27
Time revolves around me
now, so attuned to my own
needs that no force disrupts
the power from my solar
plexus, rebounding endlessly
in my shell, one-second eternity.

4/26
A long & dark morning sees me
free to rest; the warmth,
bubbling, a curse that
wracks the muscles, crystallized
flame clawing through my core,
this paradoxical peace.

4/25
The closest I can get to
memories of exhilaration:
Highway 542 before sunrise.
Trees along the road wear
spring-green moss, a fur coat
against the cold, the long & dark night.

4/24
My left hand across the table:
neatly drops the keys, leads the way
to the door that had been opened
for me. Let their ears close
in fear to the rowdy wind,
stormy midmorning of my life.

4/23
It's my turn to spit back out
the poison, externalize how sick
it feels to know my word is
worthless—a power no one has
learned to control, it breaks the
glass of illusion, clatters the teeth.

4/22
I'm standing behind this counter and
a scorpion is poised to strike, a
total stranger bent on rising
the tide of crisis, & it's all I can
do to harden the eyes, smooth the
ripples of heat in my glassy guise.

4/21
Awareness of the option to
wake up from the dream
usually comes after the zenith
of disaster, but the fog is not
lifting, Reality: going nowhere. The
ancestors' anger: still growing.

4/20
No sun quite as blinding
as the gold corona behind your
back, as I blink to be sure that
I really see you: beyond my garden
fence, across the counter where
my call meets your response.

4/19
With the space getting thicker
by the minute, I must
admit I'd rather burn at both ends
and hear a response when I call
your name, than fear the spark
and hear nothing at all.

5/12/21

Rain on your birthday again this year. The sky a slate mist, the blue tones rinsing away, a scratchy blanket on which I project memories of peach. The sunrise show is out of play. Dandelion corona that illuminates us from behind: creamy today like beeswax & coconut. The pedal sinks down; the mountains fade in: long jagged cobalt shadow.

From my new house, the same spectacular bay view that saw you freeze when that knock hit your apartment door. The phone call had come from beneath the floor. It was mostly white loggers and bandits who expelled the Chinese from here in 1884. As to who expelled you in 2020: the cops, the courts, and the ones you had called "friend" before. Between the landlords, the white liberals, and the lushes, I don't know what keeps me here anymore.

From about Bender Road until the road bends, and the flat green dairy farms re-emerge. Someone is tailing me relentlessly. Through my window, a breeze: musk, rose, oiled cedar, lilac, azalea, pine smoke, all held down with water. Here the forest claims her territory over the Nooksack Valley: rolling hills, brambles and arbors inside a bowl of mountains.

Butter-flowered shrub climbing up the power line. The lilacs, ubiquitous invaders, already beginning to shrivel from the harsh face of spring. I park and clip what blooms remain, dangling over the street side of someone's tight wooden fence. Too late to make lilac brew by now. A reminder that we must always say goodbye to our guests. Giant tree with blossoms watching over mossy corridors.

Patiently we twist up the very last strands, my left hand fingers nimble but stiff. It did take me a long time to get this good at braiding. The sunlight dazzled behind your back, baked the plaited mass of gold at my crown. That was the last time I saw you, the welcome several hours overstayed. The space had become so thick with invisible electricity.

the best of the northwest

it's actually the cold Nashville
hot chicken plucked from Safeway's deli,
while 15 more rotisserie birds waste
away, unwanted in the warmer behind me.
This chicken is not served with a thick,
tangy pickle slice, but its patient refrigeration
saves me a walk to and from the restaurant, bookends
to an already brief lunch break, or the danger
of smudging my lipstick should I dare to
savor a saucy barbeque plate by loving
hands made—the bootlicker coworker taps her
nails as I race the wind and rain to finish
my mid-day joint and pivot, then, to
chicken, working-class gourmet. This delightfully
cold hot chicken, I chomp in the dim break
room, like a goblin—sometimes, for a treat, even
microwaving it first, which does increase
the sweetness of relief, the silky taste of grease,
without ever betraying memories of salt and
honey, spicy cravings—what's really on my palate—
red-stained fingers, gleaming napkin crumpled
like money in tip jars, starting part two of this shift.

O cold hot chicken, your breading is
not crunchy, not crisp with buttermilk,
corn starch, cayenne. You do not recall
pecans, nor hardwood smoke, nor paprika,
or any flavor that might open Otohime's
box of ages, the generations of struggle,
and love, forbidden from entering my
psyche upon devouring this chicken.
No shitty well drink needed to quench
echoes of longing in my dad's voice
as he describes his ex-father-in-law:
"Your Grandpa *Bà* was a great cook."
At the Safeway self-checkout I can buy
cold hot chicken in total silence until

I go broke, unlike at the *Sìchuān* dumpling
truck—even if I was so bold as to stammer
Wǒ yào shí gè jīròu jiǎozi, I'm appalled
by not understanding the auntie's response.
Look, I gotta go back to work after this,
and you never tempt me, cold hot chicken,
with award-winning quirky cocktail menus
on the restaurant's brick wall, nor
do you drip red like *Lǎo Gān Mā* down
my family tree, you do not awaken an
ancient lexicon, do not call me to dip out at
sunrise and clip lilacs for my brew; you
are so merciful in this way, you are
passed down by disgruntled deli employees,
you have no grandmother from the
old country who gave your recipe.

Yes, belovèd be this cold Nashville hot
chicken from Safeway, the toe tapping if
one insists on purchasing fresh, not once will
pickle juice brine its flesh, devoid of
that soft moisture that won over this
town's tongues, the awards jubilee bloated
with tables: free-flowing wine and
accolades lavished upon local white-collar
bell-bottom bandits, yuppie robber barons
who will buy the engraved plaque for
an extra hundred bucks, who will wax
poetic in the magazine article about how
they wrote this recipe (they've never even
been to Tennessee); the hot dog stand guy,
at least, admits his sausages come from Costco;
the *karaage* shop guy, absent from the
splendor, and I remember when Panda Express
won best orange chicken in the Inlander,
what an eyesore that seemed, compelling me
to walk east from work to the restaurant to pick up
the chicken that could not have existed without
grandmothers in the South, church breakfasts and

cookouts, and chains, stains on history, and the latest
chef in the line himself erased, maligned,
replaced by triumphant white faces posing
against the bay view, the excitement subdued,
the semicircle Salish Sea shoreline scarred
by logging and mining, refining, and my car
in the Safeway parking lot, and the
restaurant, and the settlers seated to dine.

Absolutely none of that comes to mind upon eating
this cold hot chicken: traditions of large and
small hands together, family kitchens distilled
to ingredients on a sticker—even Safeway's
deli guards secrets like sacred gastronomy
from the ancestors, their anger, and their
life-giving love—you called out for both—
your coworkers tried everything short
of racial slurs to depose you—no one
answered the phone, nothing left but old
photos holding your gaze like a mirror, praying
your face takes after one but not the other,
meanwhile I'm walking from work to
the restaurant, spot your back behind
the dive bar's window—I go on, pacing downtown's
four-block fishbowl, each of us an eager gossip dish
which I resist, though famished; I'm sick to know
that I told you, quote: "wait for a contract
before sharing that recipe." The last two hundred years
on this land proved that plea useless, reminder
dismissed to fill my belly with Safeway's cold hot
chicken: mediocre, meaningless, nearly guilt-free.

the view from 12th st

Fog subdues the city,
the Salish Sea,
what's left of you and me
is a smothering wall of white—
noir in the night,
and navy in the first light of morning,
the honey, blush, mauve receding
into memory like old bruises,
wounds that we cover in fear
& I could almost forget
century-old Chinese-American bones
buried under Harris Avenue,
the 12th and McKenzie corner
where they took you: the view
from my new house, the
clouds of ignorance seek
the lowest places, the
fragile illusion, like skin
stretched over soymilk,
the cuts and scrapes on
your face. The smashed-in corner
of her car. The many,
many holes in the walls.
After two days of fog, I
don't see them at all.
Could almost forget the house
down the street where we met,
the beach where we stayed up
on a cold midsummer night, the
miserable wreck we were back then.
A cold heart with toes on the edge,
a walking weapon, bare hands
on legs, is that how you felt?
A demon with bloody footprints,
a mist swallowing teetering ships,
a genius with a knife and a flame,
whose lover hardens the eyes,

who tries, after three days of fog
to remember the boardwalk at Boulevard
where you wandered before you
knew me—like the future,
blocked from sight, disappearing
in the frosty white, closed
in by solid air, a corridor of cloud,
the world beyond two railings reduced
to a blank void, faint pink
and blue lights beyond a
scratchy blanket and no
earthly way to get there—
the obscured otherworld, the
opposite of the train horn,
the ears closed to alarm,
the city subdued with stillness.

5/12/22

I have lilacs out my windows
again; lilacs wilting on my
table again. Last time I made
my lilac brew, you were here;
we drank each other then, and
I can't open the jar since.
The comfort found in someone
else's embrace, the collateral damage
from our ancestors' anger, the
poison we spat at each other: how
easily distrust corrodes our love.
Conveniently you fall asleep, or
the phone disconnects, when I try
to enumerate my regrets.
I was supposed to be at SeaTac,
weary and confused, with a fire
clawing through my belly, my
deep core—a reminder that time
revolves around me now. I pass
my keys across the table. I
twist up the very last strands.
From the tiny airplane window, my
waterfront house, five minutes from
where we met, five hours aloft to
where you are now—three years since I
went this far from shore, tempted not to go
back anymore, back to the crossfaded
fools, the disposable tools of labor
we were then. Might not go back to
the professions that keep us afloat,
either—the team of five awaiting my
tide to flow back in; all three waters,
like love, seeking the lowest places.
The closest I can get to
memories of exhilaration, facing east,
the sun alight behind your back.

I want to have stolen moments with you now; to be imperfect strangers falling in love all over again, every time we meet in a new city. I want you to call me and share your joy, your pain, your weariness. I want to build a bank of memories that people would write stories about with you. I want to see you in the little free time we might have, given our lives and trajectory.

In the next five years, I want you to figure out why you keep running away, because I fell in love with you literally the day I met you, and everyone else has fallen woefully short compared to you.

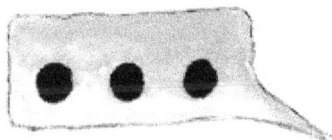

● ● ●

Asyia Gover is a writer, artist, educator, and mediator. Her poetry has appeared in the multimedia collection, *SEXT* (boys who like butterflies, 2011), and anthology zines such as *Love and Outrage* (2016). She has written and co-directed three stage plays for youth performers, in partnership with Odyssey Middle School. She has taught individual and group classes to all age levels on subjects including cannabis culture, critical pedagogy, and creative language. Her work seeks to capture a queer, third-culture perspective on ordinary life and folk traditions.

She and her feline familiar, Cora, have made a home in the liminal space between eastern and western Washington State. Depending on the season, you might find her harvesting fruits and veggies from the backyard garden, walking along the beach at low tide, curled up with a good book, or spinning donuts in a snowy parking lot.

East Side Solitude is her first chapbook. Find more of Asyia's work at www.asyias.poetry.blog.

www.ingramcontent.com/pod-product-compliance
Lightning Source LLC
Chambersburg PA
CBHW022055080426
42734CB00009B/1361